The Goal Chaser's Guide

To

Clinical Practice

Lakeeya Homsey, LICSW

TABLE OF CONTENTS

ABOUT THE AUTHOR

Lakeeya Natasha is a Licensed Independent Clinical Social Worker (LICSW), therapist, author, motivational speaker and life coach. Lakeeya holds an Associate's degree in Behavioral Health and Human Sciences (BHHS) from the Community College of Philadelphia and both Bachelor's and Master's degrees in Social Work from Temple University.

Determined to not let her beginning dictate her ending, Lakeeya used her experiences as a little girl from the inner city, to create a platform to inspire other at-risk populations to work hard and dream big. She began the process of regaining her power by telling the truth about her childhood abusers. Having adults in her life making unhealthy choices and not being supported when she came forward, left her vulnerable to other predators and lead to years of untreated mental health issues including several suicide attempts. Lakeeya recognized no one would give her the freedom she longed for so she fought for it and claimed it as hers. Having good and consistent talk therapy and redefining her relationship with God is how she fought back. She fights back those thoughts of inadequacy and victimhood daily. She shares that hope with all she comes in contact with whether in a group home, homeless shelters, office settings or the Philadelphia Prison System. All of her clients learn that freedom is not a place; it is a mindset.

After recovering from a toxic and abusive first marriage and unhappy with the dating scene she got marriage for the second time. Recognizing she craved the stability that marriage could bring to her children and her desire to be a "good wife", Lakeeya became the CEO and co-founder of the Love Train Experience. The organization demonstrates the reality of marriage and promotes happy, healthy relationships. From 2013 to 2019, the Love Train has hosted eight committed couple retreats, six adult game nights and countless date night outs events. The goal of the organization was simple "to have more people choose healthy partnerships and to make commitment fun." Unfortunately, and fortunately, working with other couples, she realized that though her second marriage was not abusive, it was definitely toxic, because she was left lonely and vulnerable by a man that said he was her husband. She began 2020, as a newly separated woman yet again and decided it was best to discontinue her work with the Love Train because the work, she did with other couples, was not a reflection her own relationship.

Lakeeya knows from both personal and professional experiences that 1) acknowledging one has a problem is the hardest step to healing and 2) finding healthy support and accountability partner is the second. She launched her own private practice with this in mind.

Transitions4Life, LLC offers mobile and e-therapy (text, call, email, and video) to minimize excuses from busy working professionals. Through Transitions4Life, Lakeeya assist individuals, families, couples, and other helping professionals in becoming more aware of specific patterns that are keeping them stuck and preventing them from moving forward. She provides the tools and strategies that women and men need to overcome their obstacles to live their best lives and define their version of freedom.

Along with private clinical practice, Lakeeya used the tips in her small book series to become one of the youngest and highest paid clinical supervisors of a large non-profit community mental health agency. Covid-19 shifted how everyone did business and because Transitions4Life was already set up as a telehealth practice, it took off and surpassed its financial benchmarks. Having great organization and drive, Lakeeya was able to maintain and grow her practice of one while working full time for the other organization. That all changed suddenly.

In March 2021, as she was on medical leave, she received a call from the HR department saying she was terminated. She found out a few weeks later, that the company went into bankruptcy and closed. Having her own business already, she was taken back emotionally but not knock down financially. That experience solidified the notion that jobs are not loyal to no one but itself and we as a people need to be loyal to ourselves, our purpose, and people attached to us over any job. Additionally, it became even more important for Lakeeya Natasha to help others succeed in business even if it is just a secondary income because this Post Pandemic life brings so much uncertainty.

Lakeeya credits her faith in God for her ability to push past her pain to find her purpose. She understands that her life and her story are not her own. They are meant to be shared to set others held captive free.

This story has a happy ending, for she finally found her person! She married her best friend and new business partner, Walter Homsey, on May 24, 2022. Both are licensed therapists wanting to help people find personal freedom through connection with their higher selves, nature, and re-establishing sense of community. They created a platform to do just that called One Trip Over the Moon. Through One Trip Over the Moon, the couple offers a holistic approach to healing and embracing peace and joy.

For more information about **Transitions4Life, LLC,** please contact: askkeeya@gmail.com or follow us on Facebook & Instagram.

For more information about **One Trip Over the Moon, LLC,** contact onetripoverthemoon@gmail.com or follow us on Facebook, Instagram, & Twitter

INTRODUCTION: SHIFTING MINDSETS

You could have just graduated from school or may have years of experience, but you have a burning desire to do more and be more in your field of practice. You may have a financial goal to make a six or seven figure salary or be your own boss with a thriving practice. Whatever your desire or goal, welcome to the Goal Chasers Club!

When you go to school for the humanities: sociology, psychology, criminal justice or social work, people will assume that your income is limited. When people think of someone who says "I want to be a doctor or a lawyer", they are more likely to think those people have unlimited income potential.

I have learned over the years that that mindset is far from the truth. The income potential for every person is limitless. Our circumstances may create barriers, but we create the limits. We create the narrative of lack, and when you operate from that narrative, you produce lack.

When you are ready to operate out of your abundance, you will achieve your abundance. You are your first and most important client. So, I ask you to think about, "What are YOUR goals and dreams? What is YOUR plan to achieve those things you desire? What are YOUR barriers to the success you seek? Who can you partner to support you in ensuring YOUR success?" Write down the answers to these questions, create a plan ad move forward. Even if you are scared…START!

If you have the desire, if you see the vision…it is not a coincidence that your natural gifts and talents align with your vision. We are come hardwired with all of the tools we need to succeed in our purpose. So, why do so many of us struggle to walk in our purpose? Comparisons!

We compare our purpose and the way we do things to others. We make the false assumption that they we all have the same trajectory. When we compare our failures and successes to others which sometimes develops into professional paralysis. We allow ourselves to remain stuck in jobs (and other life roles) that are not fulfilling or challenging but "safe".

I have a question, "Are you safe in mediocrity?" This doesn't mean you have to have a desire just to have more. There is nothing wrong with being content with what you have if it is true job contentment (which is the ultimate goal for any professional).

However, if you are experiencing restlessness and frustration in your current situation that is your mind, body and soul are screaming at you ***"You are capable of more and there is more for the taking!"***

No matter how old you are, you have something to offer the world in a way that only you can. Don't deprive us of your presence and your presents, your gifts. Prepare to make your mark, and don't worry about who believes in your dreams. ***You can show people better than you can tell them!***

This small book series includes best practice highlights, promotes self-care, and encourages entrepreneurship. I initially created my small book series with the intent to help new counselors and potentially burned-out counselors with tips and strategies to overcome the worst (but most important) part of our jobs – PAPERWORK!

Paperwork and compassion fatigue are the top non-monetary reasons why great people leave the field prematurely. Yet it was decided in the past 20 years, with the rise of managed care and healthcare bureaucracy, that the only way to measure the value of a session was by reading a well-crafted progress note. Understanding those things, I realized it would be a great opportunity to help industry professionals in these areas as well.

The phrase "goal chaser" is intentionally mentioned throughout the book. The term is not often used to describe counselors, social workers or case managers. However, it does apply since a goal chaser is a person who has a dream or vision and goes for it all by creating a strategic action plan.

Each step of the plan is an objective that leads to a time sensitive goal. Each goal gets the person closer to the actualization of their overall dream or vision. With each accomplished goal, a person develops increased confidence that their pursuit (chase) of the next goal will also be fruitful.

A goal chaser has a distinguished mindset that separates them from others in the same profession. A goal chaser doesn't settle on just making it (or making excuses), they set out to crush every challenge, overcome every barrier and never accept "no" as a denial to their dreams. They ultimately win at life by staying committed to their purpose for the long haul.

At age 24, my mindset was shifted unexpectedly. I was a newly single (pending divorce) mother of two. I was an unemployed college dropout who had to move back in with my parents to restart my life and rebuild my credit. My father found me a job at a local deli, and I applied for food stamps and childcare assistance.

I attempted to register for college the year before, but I had two student loans in default so was denied financial aid. I settled one loan and made a payment arrangement for the second one. After six months of making consistent payments, in 2006, I was able to enroll as a part-time student at the Community College of Philadelphia (CCP).

I thought for many years that my first class "Introduction to Helping Professionals" changed my life. Now, I understand that class was a tool for the Creator to remind me who I was, a goal chaser. It put me back on track towards the life I was born to live.

The instructor was a young African American female, Dr. Hickman. Dr. Hickman was a Licensed Clinical Social Worker (LCSW). In the first class, she said something so simple but yet profound "Don't let anyone tell you how much money you can make. You can make as much money as you want, and don't let anyone tell you social workers don't make money!"

In that class, as a broke, single mother of two on welfare my heart jumped. I believed her! I believed in me. It reminded me of a memory I had as a small child when I heard a voice tell me I would be a millionaire. I had forgotten about that voice until I was sitting in that class and heard those heard those words from Dr. Hickman. Instantly, a shift took place in my life. I didn't win the lottery, but I won an abundant mindset.

Abundance isn't free. Dr. Hickman pushed me hard. I received many papers back with red ink all over them. It was a challenge which I accepted enthusiastically. I began attending college full-time and graduated in 2008 from the Community College of Philadelphia with high honors AND received the Behavioral Health and Human Services (BHHS) Founding Faculty Award.

With Dr. Hickman's words in my ear and a new sense of faith and confidence, I set my next educational goals: Bachelor's degree by 2010 and Master's degree by 2012. During that time, I began working as a paraprofessional in the human services field and no longer received government benefits. I worked and went to school full-time and moved me and my babies to our own small apartment.

I wanted more for my children, and I felt like I had something to prove to everyone who didn't think it was possible. So, I graduated cum laude from Temple University in both programs in May 2012. I walked across the stage of the Liacouras Center with a Master's degree in Social Work with a concentration in Health/Mental Health. With that, I had my first license under my belt. I was a licensed social worker. The first step to become a LCSW in the state of

Pennsylvania.

In 2014, I remarried and while pregnant with my third child, I passed my board exam and received the title I had been chasing since 2006. I officially became a Licensed Clinical Social Worker (LCSW). As of June 2022, I am now licensed in Pennsylvania, Delaware, New Jersey, and Massachusetts.

I have increased my income every year I have been a social worker. Don't get me wrong, there is nothing wrong with having a side business that is not related to social work or therapy. However, I almost fell into the trap of thinking that the only way to hit my financial goals was to tap into "more lucrative" industries.

That thinking is a myth. With Covid stress, growing awareness of mental illness, and the self-care movement, helping professionals are in higher demand. There is a shortage of culturally competent and ethnically diverse professionals. So, mental health providers are able to demand higher salaries as well as begin their own organizations, private practices, and consulting businesses.

I don't share my story to boast. I share to encourage you. Each of us has an amazing story of overcoming, surviving and thriving. No story is greater or lesser than another, and each story can be leveraged to advance our work in the field. I know most of us do not get into this field for the money; that doesn't mean there is not money to be made.

With set goals in the forefront of our minds, difficult days become bearable. The best way to navigate this field and to have a long, successful career is to have a game plan from the beginning which should include these components:

- Hold yourself just as accountable as you expect your clients to be

- Keep up with your paperwork

- Establish a good work/life balance

- Always leave time to work on your goals and dreams

Thank you for doing an often-thankless job. I hope this small book series is useful to your practice. Good luck in your future endeavors as a member of the Goal Chaser's Club!

TIP #1: THERAPY STARTS AND ENDS WITH YOU

I often tell reluctant clients that "therapy is like dating". It is all about chemistry and connection (unlike in dating, beware of sexual chemistry of course).

You may have to start and stop with a few counselors before you find the right one and that is all a part of the process. Just like dating, both parties come with their own agenda and the struggle is to find a way for both agendas to be validated because if one or both agendas are not validated as important, the relationship tends to fade.

The pairing process (therapeutic alliance) gives a way for the client and counselor to learn more about themselves and what they need to be their best selves. Don't take it personal, if a client is resistant or down right refuses to see you.

On the other hand, don't be hard on yourself, if you realize you don't like to work with certain populations or you cringe if you see a certain client's name on your schedule for the day. Discuss either scenario in clinical supervision as it will help your growth as a cultural-competent, person-centered, strength-based clinician.

We all have our dream partner created in our mind. After being in the field for a while, you begin to develop your dream client. We may find that we work well with people of the same sex or opposite sex, people of a certain age, people of a certain religious or cultural background, or people with a certain diagnosis.

Often as a new counselor, we can't pick and choose our caseload yet that doesn't mean we don't have a preference. As we pay our dues in the field and work in various settings with various populations, we ultimately find our niche and settle in.

It is vital for your longevity in the helping field that you strive to find your niche. Normally, you know that it is your niche when it relates to 1) your passion and 2) the groups of people that you would work with for free if you had too, such as: women and children, the LGBT-Q community, the growing elderly population in need of mental health care, or minorities. These populations continue to be in need of great providers.

There are endless possibilities for you to make an

impact. To make a positive impact, you must bring you're A-game to every session.

How to Make Sure You are Bringing You're A-Game

- **Be Present in Every Session** Don't be distracted by computers, phones, food or drink, or any other non-related tasks when a client is opening up to you

- **Listen Intently** for your client's answers to their own problems. Pay particular attention to the hidden, deeper under the surface responses.

- **Ask** what people, places, and things helped them and hurt them before. Use the information to guide your treatment planning.

- **Set Boundaries and Expectations from Session 1** The things that trip counselors up the most are: scheduling and cancelling appointments, how to address late clients, payments, and limits to confidentiality.

- **Be Prepared for Every Session** mentally, physically, and emotionally. *NOTE: If you are sick, grieving or preoccupied with your personal life you are not 100% present. If you are struggling with any of these things,* *it is important to utilize good self-care, seek clinical supervision, take time off, and find a therapist for extra support.*

- **<u>Be Genuine</u>** Express genuine validation, concern, and affirmation.

- **<u>Use Evidence Based Therapeutic Techniques</u>** as tools **<u>not</u>** rules. Sessions should not be robotic or rehearsed. Clients are coming to you as an expert. So, use learned strategies that have been proven to work yet leave room for the client to define what they need from you as a provider.

- **<u>Be Flexible to Accommodate Your Client's HERE AND NOW</u>** For example, from the last session you may have developed a plan for what to discuss next or what paperwork to complete. Remember, clients are human beings whose lives change in the blink of an eye. Leave room to discuss what is **important to them now** versus what they said was important in a prior session.

- **<u>Say No</u>** to cases that trigger you, or you don't feel trained enough to properly treat the client. In the cases where you don't feel you have the expertise to treat the client, seek additional clinical supervision.

- **<u>Document every session</u>** Fundamentally, a therapist note should be thought of as a legal document and everything that is contained in the should be able to be answered by the author while under oath. For this and a myriad of other reasons, it is important to be circumspect regarding documentation. Certain mental health organizations need specific information in notes to justify payment yet if you have your own practice, the more concise the better. (Check out my book *Progress Notes Made Simple* if this is an area of concern)

- **<u>Self-Care is MANDATORY, Not Optional</u>** Self-Care for Mental Health Professionals 101:

  - Don't apologize or feel guilty that you need to care for yourself first. As the saying goes, "You can't pour from an empty cup".

  - Get good sleep.

  - Eat a balance diet.

  - Exercise or participate in a physical hobby at least once a week.

  - **Say NO** to things that don't feel good to you, or don't support positive energy for you.

- Don't overbook yourself.

- Don't let paperwork overwhelm you. Unless you work from home, use time management and organization strategies to minimize paperwork at home. (If you do work from home, try to use a specific space and a specific time to complete paperwork.)

- Join groups with likeminded people for emotional support and professional accountability.

- Use your clinical supervision time to advance your skills and grow. Be prepared with topics to discuss.

- Keep dreaming **AND** working on your dreams.

- Take personal and mental health days without shame.

- Get your Continuing Education Units (CEUs) in topics that interest you, and go to conferences/retreats when you can.

- Get your own therapist. Every counselor should go through the therapy process at least once. However, regular check ins with a therapist maintains good mental health just as regular check ins with our physician help maintain our physical health.

TIP #2: KNOW YOUR CLIENT AND THEIR WANTS

I have learned over the years that all clients come to us knowing what they want and *most* know how to get there. People go to therapy for one of two reasons: To change or to stay the same. In that conceptual framework, I have found that there are three types of clients seeking help:

1. The client who lost their way and forgot what they innately want:

   a. Mandated referrals
   b. Court commitments
   c. Clients in the Pre-Contemplation Stage of Change

2. The client who knows their wants but needs direction:

   a. Clients struggling with sobriety
   b. Newly diagnosed clients
   c. Returning clients

      d. Clients in the Contemplation and Preparation Stages of Change

3. The client who knows what they want, knows what they need to do to get it but needs an accountability partner:

      a. People diagnosed with Chronic/Severe Mental Illness or SMI
      b. Couples/Families
      c. Clients in the Action and Maintenance Stages of Change

Of course, every client is an individual with unique life experiences, stressors, dreams and barriers to the life they truly want. Therefore, personalized treatment is a must for success. However, structured activities, interventions and homework are still beneficial for each type of client.

I have included at the end of the book, two of the activities/homework I used for rapport building to begin treatment planning for the individual (or family).

ACTIVITY 1: "THE CHANGES I WANT TO MAKE" HANDOUT

This activity can be either be worked on together during the first two sessions or given has homework in the first session to review in the second session.

The handout allows clients to explore what do they really want by having them choose only two things they want to change. This allows them to focus on what is most important and how changing those two things will ultimately benefit them and/or their relationships. By writing down long term and short-term goals, identifying support people as well as barriers, and defining time frame for change- the client has done the hard part for you. By completing this handout, they created their own treatment plan!

You now have a reference point for future sessions and can use this form to determine if your client or your sessions on track for the intended goals.

This handout can be used for long term clients as well after they resolved the initial reason for coming to therapy, they often build self-efficacy and greater desire to tackle of additional challenges.

ACTIVITY 2: "LET ME INTRODUCE MYSELF" HANDOUT

This activity can be used when you were not the counselor that completed the client's intake or if the case was transferred to you. This is a way to give the client a clean slate and for you to make a positive impression. It also provides you an opportunity to collect important information that is not always in the client intake paperwork.

You can use the handout as is or you can add your own questions. This is joining activity so refrain from processing any one answer at this time and just listen. *Unconditional Positive Regard*, *Acceptance*, and *Validation* are essential for a successful therapeutic relationship. Be leary to express judgement or over correct in beginning sessions before gaining your client's trust.

TIP #3: CHASE YOUR GOALS AS YOU WORK WITH AND FOR OTHERS

Very few people in human services graduate from school and start their own business without prior experience in the field. Before branching off into their own ventures, most people have experienced/recognized service gaps, lack of utilization as well as resource deficiencies in their respective fields by first working within the flawed systems.

While working for a company or companies, be on high alert for areas that you and your services would be needed and appreciated once you venture out on your own. Your successful private practice will need the skills you developed at your current and former places of employment as well as the information you glean from seasoned professionals while employed by these places.

It's important not to wait until you have your own practice to carry yourself as a boss. Treat yourself as your own employee. Give yourself deadlines and high expectations. While your employer benefits from your dedication and professionalism, build the personal accountability every independent contractor, private practice owner, nonprofit president and company CEO should have to truly call themselves successful.

By doing this, you may find yourself getting promotions, raises and bonuses at your "traditional" job. These things can be either a perk to enjoy for the moment or an obstacle to your branching out on your own because you get "comfortable" where you are.

It has become apparent that people need precipitating factors to leave a job. Normally, you don't leave a job where you are happy. It is usually because you feel undervalued, underutilized, overworked, or under paid. The workplace may be drama-filled or no one is available to give you the proper supervision for you to expand your clinical skills and practicum. These are usually the barriers that become our greatest motivation to work on our dreams.

What if the barriers are not there or are not obvious? You may be restless and desire more, but there is nothing pushing you to move. This is where I challenge anyone and everyone desiring something different to step out on their own. Do it but do it smart!

Very few of us have the money or resources to up and quit our jobs and start a new venture. We have things like bills, families, student loans and other obligations. We also shouldn't make our transitions out of frustration. We must have a deliberate plan to act upon, and often times that plan has to be worked on while we work for someone else.

Give your job the best you have to offer. Then, pay yourself back by giving YOUR dreams the best YOU have to offer. Remember, in most cases, your supervisor, boss or CEO is where they are because he or she believed in their dreams. You cannot continue to work on someone else's dream and not give yours a chance. You do not need anyone to cosign your vision. It was given to YOU. As you operate in your vision, people will be put in your path that will help you bring your vision to life.

You don't need money or resources to start. It costs nothing to write down your dreams and action steps. Money will come as you work through your plan. You don't need your family and friends to believe in you for you to be successful. It is nice to hear from a loved one that they can see your vision, but it is not a prerequisite to success. Your genuine supporters will emerge with perfect timing. Trust the process!

Sometimes failure can be your friend, but fear cannot. The next leaders of the world are lurking in the shadows paralyzed by their fear of failure. Recognize that it is ok to try and fail. All of the "greats" usually have a story of a failure but was it really failure if they ended up exactly where they belong. Most of us can think of a celebrity we admire who speaks about a story of struggle or of failure before their big break.

Every failure is an opportunity to learn, grow and regroup. Things may not work out on your first attempt, but once you find success, you will realize those early failures were your friends. It is fear that is the enemy. Fear will make you feel like you are not worthy of your dreams. Fear will make you feel like you are not good enough to follow through with your plans. Fear will make you settle for less than what is intended for you. Fear is a liar. The truth is that fear is scared of you, your power and your ability to diminish its presence in your life and those around you.

Stop comparing yourself to others. There may be millions of people writing books, but no one has your story…so write! There may be millions of people delivering motivational videos and speeches, but no one has your message…so speak! There may be millions of people starting private practices, but not one of them can service your clients like you can.so build that practice! Be you, and what is yours will come to you.

Now, you are at Point A and you can see your Point B clear as day. Neither Point A nor Point B is the problem. The problem is becoming discouraged before you even start making positive change or start moving from Point A to Point B. Don't become one of the people who talks themselves into believing their Point A is too far away or their Point B is to grand.

As already stated, neither point is the problem. The problem is an innate fear of failure. It paralyzes us. We want to choose the exact perfect route before we make a move. As famously stated by Voltaire, "Perfect is the enemy of the good." Push back your imposter syndrome and remind yourself, daily if needed, that you are already good enough. Every successful person, successful business owner or person with "Cinderella story" will tell you "There are no wrong paths." Each path will lead you to Point B if you allow, expect and prepare for obstacles. Perfect your ability to regroup and be flexible.

Take baby steps, take several steps forward, take a leap of faith. It doesn't matter what you do…just start moving in the direction of your goals! Trust the process, and don't stop no matter how long it takes to get to Point B. It will happen as long as you can see it in front of you. Whatever you can see, you have the ability to create. You are a Goal Chaser!

Don't forget:

1. To CTRL+ALT+DEL when needed:

- **Control yourself**- understand what is inside and outside of your control

- **Alter your thinking**- know that if it has been done many times or never been done before doesn't change the fact you can create your own way towards success

- **Delete negativity**- you should limit anything and anyone that is hindering your personal growth and professional progress

  - Limit or Stop interactions with unsupportive family and friends

    - Replace with smaller circle of support- this can be one circle or several different circles (I personally have different groups of friends for various reasons- some people overlap yet most don't and that is completely okay)

  - Block, Unfriend, or Unfollow people from social media that cause you distress or make you question your value in a particular space

- My rule is "if it doesn't inspire, it must expire"

  o Eliminate your bad habits- you know, the things that bring you shame, guilt, or remorse. Sometimes we are our worst enemy. We have to hold ourselves accountable as much as we want our clients to.

Don't forget:

2. You Can:

- Start Late- no age limit for success

- Start Over-no limit on the number of times to restart or start over

- Be Unsure- you don't have to know every thing before you start, learn as you go

- Act Differently- there will be people that will say you have changed or you are acting different, let them talk because to be successful you would have to change AND this change is for the better

- Try and fail- Failure in the Present is a Lesson in the Future. As long as you don't give up, you will never fail (Try different things, Try new things, Try, Try, Try- all things won't work but all worth a try)

You can do these things and STILL succeed!

TIP #4: DON'T LET DOCUMENTATION BEAT YOU

Paperwork. Just saying it and writing down the word makes me cringe. I don't know if any counselor who likes it: intakes, assessment summaries, recovery plans, treatment plans, safety plans, progress notes, group notes, discharge summaries and court reports.

We did not get into this field to do paperwork, but some days, it is all we do. Paperwork can consume our lives. Many counselors complete paperwork on their days off, during family time and even during vacation. We all know that paperwork is the way we secure our payments and often times keeps us employed. However, it doesn't make it any easier to complete.

Documentation does not have to get the best of you. Quitting a job because of the paperwork is not good practice, because the next job will also have its fair share of documenting. No one should be obligated to complete paperwork for no pay, but it is an integral part of our jobs. There are ways to set yourself up so that documentation won't beat you.

First, gain an understanding of every document in your organization. If there are any redundant forms or processes, discuss them with your supervisor. There may be a way to integrate documents that hadn't been considered before. However, if you are told there is a good reason for similar forms to be completed for one client, ask your supervisor for further explanation to gain a better understanding. (Most likely, it can be related to billing for services.)

Second, use good time management and organization skills. I find that many of my colleagues that struggle with paperwork are the ones who wait until the end of the day (or worse the end of the week) to complete their notes. Save a few minutes at the even of the session to review with the client what was discussed and plan for the next appointment. Write everything down immediately. Once the client leaves the office, spend a few minutes finishing the notes.

Lastly, understand what is required for good notes. Learn the structure and then create templates for general topics and assessments. This will cut down on your time rewriting similar notes. Appendix C is a handout I created (Good Notes Have Good Structure) for those I supervise to that they can understand the structure of good notes.

DISCLAIMER:

There are many other manuals and workbooks out there that can help you get started with Cognitive Behavioral Therapy (CBT). I have provided some resources in Appendix D.

This e-book doesn't review the therapeutic process and strategies for the work within a session, so Appendix D also includes some tools if you feel stuck or don't quite remember CBT interventions to use during your sessions. CBT is not the only useful mode of treatment, so I encourage you to discover what treatment modalities work best for you and your client population.

I hope this book, along with the others in the series, helps you in your quest of becoming a Goal Chaser!

All Currently Available on Kindle and Amazon

- Progress Notes Made Simple by Lakeeya Homsey, LICSW

- Treatment Planning Made Simple by Lakeeya Homsey, LICSW

- I Quit! A Book about Burnout by Walter Homsey, LCSW and Lakeeya Homsey, LICSW

APPENDIX A

The Changes I Want to Make Activity
Handout

INSTRUCTIONS: Write down two things you would like to change. Grab a notebook and something to write with and jot down your thoughts in as much detail as you can the statements/questions below the changes you noted. **NOTE: Don't allow yourself to get overwhelmed. All information can be discussed in session to assist with thinking the answers through.**

1. The changes I want to make are:

Change #1

____

____

____

____

____

Change #2

____

____

____

____

____

____

2. The most important reasons I want to make these changes are…?

3. My main goals for myself for making these changes are…?

4. The first steps (short-term objectives) I plan to take in changing are…?

5. I plan to do these things (long-term objectives) to reach my goals…

6. Some things or people that could interfere with my plan and some of strategies I can use to overcome them are…?

7. Other people can help me in changing by…?

8. I hope that my plan will have these positive results…

9. I will know if my plan is working if…?

APPENDIX B

Let Me Re-Introduce Myself Activity Handout

INSTRUCTIONS: If you could re-introduce yourself after implementing the changes you seek, what would that look like? Grab a notebook and something to write with and jot down your thoughts in as much detail as you can after "re-introducing" yourself. **NOTE: Don't allow yourself to get overwhelmed. All information can be discussed in session to assist with thinking the answers through.**

1. My full name is _______________________________

2. I am also known by _______________________________

3. Three things you wouldn't know by looking at me are…

    1. _______________________________

    2. _______________________________

    3. _______________________________

1. My guilty pleasures are…

2. My pet peeves are…

3. What I seek in a counselor is…

4. My greatest challenges/weaknesses/struggles are…

5. The top ways I relieve stress are…

6. My dream job is…

7. My 3-5 year plan includes…

8. What do you want to gain from counseling (the first six months)?

9. What do you hope to gain from counseling long term (over six months)?

APPENDIX C

Good Notes Have Good Structure

DIRP (Data, Intervention, Response, Plan)

or DAP (Data, Assessment, Plan) Notes

There are other popular Note taking structures (i.e. SOAP note etc.) however it would not be advantageous for me to spend time writing samples of every type of note when many of these can be easily accessed online.

I will focus on the DIRP note taking process for that is the one I used mostly in community mental health settings. The only difference between **DIRP** and **DAP** is that some practices combine the **IR** into **A** for Assessment.

DATA (Observations)

- **Who, what when, where, why?** Example, Clinician met with the client in the office for an individual session. Client arrives on time and appropriately dressed for the weather.

Clinician and client reviewed progress since last appointment. Client was able to articulate positive change efforts, current stressors as well as the desire to remain emotionally stable. Client reports compliance with prescribed medication with symptom relief.

INTERVENTION (Techniques, Strategies, Paperwork)

- Whatever attempted or completed in a session goes here. **TIP:** If active recovery plan is available, cut and paste the interventions from the plan.

- Use interpersonal therapy techniques to explore and resolve issues surrounding grief, role disputes, role transitions and social skills deficits. Provide support and strategies for resolving identified interpersonal issues.

RESPONSE (Clinical Impression)

- What is the client's reaction to your intervention? What is your overall clinical impression?

- Stage of change, risk level, current stability

PLAN (Follow-Up)

- Next appointment, next objective to work on,

paperwork needed, homework given and any case management.

APPENDIX D

A few of many Tools and References for Clinicians (CBT Specific)

<u>Bright Futures – Tool for Professionals: Table 1: Stages of Change and Goals of Intervention</u>

<u>https://www.brightfutures.org/mentalhealth/pdf/professionals/bridges/table.pdf</u>

The CBT Toolbox: A Workbook for Clients and Clinicians by Jeff Riggenbach (<u>Amazon</u>)

Client's Guidebook: "Activities and Your Mood" by Community Partners in Care

The Cognitive Behavioral Workbook for Anxiety: A Step-by-Step Program by William J. Knaus and Jon Carlson (<u>Amazon</u>)

The Cognitive Behavioral Workbook for Depression: A Step-by-Step Program by William J.

Knaus and Albert Ellis (<u>Amazon</u>)

Cognitive-Behavioral Therapy Skills Workbook by Barry Gregory (<u>Amazon</u>)

You could have just graduated from school or may have years of experience, with the burning desire to do more and be more in your field of practice. You may have a financial goal to make a six or seven figure salary or be your own boss with a thriving practice.

I don't share my story, tips, and strategies to boast. I share to encourage you. Each of us has an amazing story of overcoming, surviving and thriving. No story is greater or lesser than another, and each story can be leveraged to advance our work in the field. I know most of us do not get into this field for the money; that doesn't mean there is not money to be made.

Whatever your desire or goal, welcome to the Goal Chaser's Club!

www.ingramcontent.com/pod-product-compliance
Lightning Source LLC
Chambersburg PA
CBHW031431250726

48656CB00002B/927